HISTORICAL PRINTS
OF AMERICAN CITIES

comments by
Larry Freeman

Century House - Watkins Glen, N. Y.

Historical Notes

The color inserts show two interesting varieties of historical views. The print of Lower Broadway, New York (1826) is typical of *interior views* made earlier than those pictured in this book. It also shows one printing establishment that was engaged in turning out such views. The print of Cleveland (1833) shows the earlier tendency in *exterior views* to get as near to the town as possible rather than convey a panoramic effect, as in typical 1850 views. Several artists and print houses made series of American views around 1850, but not a single one achieved a nation-wide depiction of the developing Union.

INTRODUCTION

So many American cities are holding centennials—or have recently held them—that a portfolio of their early views should have value and interest. What we have done here is bring together from widely scattered sources a representative sampling of the cradle places of U. S. industry and commerce, as they appeared around 1850 (with some leeway in either direction). We have also given something of the history of the print and of the subject at the time depicted.

In a project of this type, choice of subjects is a knotty problem. One is tempted to use mainly the easily available and the pictorially important prints. To do so, however, would fail to show the country-wide sweep of development a hundred years ago. Numerous print collections exist depicting the early development of towns and cities along the eastern seaboard; an entire book could be built around prints of Boston, or Philadelphia or New York. Western views, with the exception of California, are little known and hard to come by. Even the discriminating Phelps-Stokes collection at New York Public Library is notably weak on the West. So it has become our job to supplement reproductions from Phelps-Stokes with some from our own collection. Thanks is due to the print department of New York Public Library for aid and assistance in our task.

We have tried to show herein centenary views representative of cities in all 48 states of the union (see Index). This has been a little difficult for States that were Territories until long after 1850; but it has seemed to us important—at least in this survey volume—to show the breadth rather than the depth of historical print collecting. Collections like Phelps-Stokes and Garvan (Yale) already hold the rarities in 18th and early 19th century views. But there is a wealth of lithographs and steel engravings of the late 19th century that can still be acquired for the proverbial song. Many of these would be important acquisitions to an individual or a library bent on collecting early views of a given locale.

It is hoped this small volume will stimulate the collecting of *local* material, especially in the Middle and Far West. The importance of maintaining files of historical prints has long been recognized in European cities and should be encouraged in our own. Such collections stimulate civic pride as well as please the eye. Few people yet seem to realize that the individuality of towns and cities is just as pronounced and interesting as that of persons. The game of looking at pictures of the home town a hundred years ago is often the same as that of studying the group portrait of the Senior Class at Central High. Many a person is able to spot his great-grandfather's store down by the river, or his family's first home in America. And is *that* the way State Street used to look? What a get-up! Such pictures make history more vital, life more real. Their preservation becomes a treasured part of our American heritage.

LARRY FREEMAN

Freeman Farms
March 15, 1952.

3

Hartford, Conn., 1840.

An 18 x 12 colored aquatint published by Robt. Havell, 172 Fulton St., New York. This is one of a very few recorded impressions and is from the Phelps-Stokes collection. It shows the town on the Connecticut (founded 1639) as it was changing from trade to insurance and manufacturing center. The large building with cupola, in the right center, is the first state capitol, erected 1792 and used until the new capitol was erected in 1879. To the left is the steeple of the First Congregational Church, dedicated in 1807. The three square towers with pinnacles, at the right, are (left to right) First Baptist Church (1830), Episcopal Church (1827) and Trinity Roman Catholic Church (1830).

Boston, Massachusetts, 1840.

A 6 x 10 lithograph, probably taken from the Bennett acquatint entitled *Boston from City Point*. (1853). Buildings still standing include the domed State House and to its right, the cupolaed Faneuil Hall. Next to New York, Boston is probably the most delineated city in America.

Charleston, S. C., 1840.

A 6 x 9 engraving in the LADIES REPOSITORY and taken from the rare Keenan acquatint. Settlement here was begun in 1680, and soon it became the largest and wealthiest settlement south of Philadelphia. Charleston is one city that has not changed drastically with the years. Many of its early buildings, including St. Michael Episcopal Church (center of view) are still standing. The water in the foreground is the Cooper River flowing into the Atlantic Ocean.

Mobile, Ala., 1841.

Taken from the marsh opposite the city near Pinto's residence. Section from 24 x 16 acquatent by W. J. Bennett (Henry I. Megarcy, N. Y.). Founded by the French in 1710 and ceded to England in 1763, it passed into Spanish hands in 1780 and eventually seized for the United States in 1813. This waterfront view has been made practically unrecognizable by the development of the great southern port in the last few decades.

Washington, D. C., 1851.

A 27 x 17 colored lithograph by E. Sachse & Co., Baltimore, Md. In the foreground is the capitol with the newly added wings, but with the original saucer-shaped dome. In the left background is the Washington Monument showing the circular columnal porch around the base, as called for in the original design, but never carried out. To the left front of the monument is the Smithsonian Institute, begun in 1847 and still standing. The long colonnaded building, at the end of Pennsylvania Avenue and to its right, is the Treasury, begun in 1834 and remodelled shortly after this view was made. Back of the Treasury is the White House and to the left on the hill is the Naval Observatory of 1842. This seat of the Government of the United States was set up by an act of Congress in 1790, and laid out by Major L'Enfant on a plan unique in this country. The Washington City Canal which appears in the center of the view shown, was filled in after the Civil War and a tidal basin developed beyond the Washington Monument. On the hills in the right center background is Georgetown, established 1751.

Three New York State Views of 1840.

(4 x 2 drawings by J. W. Barber appearing in Our Whole Country.)

1. Lockport (founded 1821) showing the original five locks of the Erie Canal. 2. South View of Newburgh (founded 1752). Steeple at extreme left is First Presbyterian Church used by Washington in his occupation of 1782-83. Little dome on the right is Newburgh Free Academy, built about 1810. 3. Peekskill (founded 1764) with St. Peter's Church shown, where Washington conducted services for his soldiers.

Lockport. N.Y.

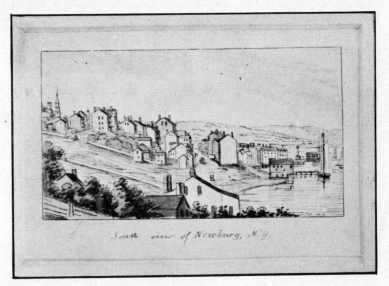

South view of Newburg, N.Y.

East view of Peekskill N.Y. 18__

Jersey City, N. J., 1860.

Taken from a ship's mast directly opposite Montgomery Street. Situated on a hook of land between the Hudson River on the east and Hackensack River on the west, Jersey City remained farm land until 1804, when the town was first laid out. Manufacturing growth came just before the Civil War. The spire in the center of view is the First Presbyterian Church, erected on Wall Street, New York City in 1835, taken down and reerected at Washington and Sussex Streets, Jersey City in 1844.

Philadelphia, Pa., 1851.

Philadelphia from Belmont. A 12 x 9 line engraving by G. Perkins. The town situated at the confluence of the Delaware and Schuykill Rivers was laid out in 1682 and was for a long time the principle city of the American colonies. Philadelphia has about as many early views as New York and Boston, but here is shown a view contemporary with other cities of this period. "Belmont" was one of the early country estates bordering the Schuykill to the west of Philadelphia (it first spread north and south along the Delaware) which were taken over by the city to form "Fairmont Park." This view looks east above the dam of the famed Fairmont Water Works, which early supplied the mains of the city, and is near the site of the 1876 Centennial Exposition.

New York, N. Y., 1848 (see page 19)

From the steeple of St. Paul's Church, looking East, South and West.
A 36 x 21 colored acquatint by Henry Papprill. Being at the very center of
the print publishing trade, New York is the most delineated city in America.
Manhattan Island, whose white settlement dates from 1625, has also gone
through the most complete and ever-changing rebuilding anywhere. This
is one of the most comprehensive and interesting views of the lower tip of
the island one hundred years ago. Brady's celebrated Daguerrian Miniature
Gallery is seen in the center foreground (southwest corner Fulton and
Broadway) and Barnum's Museum is opposite St. Paul's (southeast corner
Broadway and Ann Street). Of the four churches shown (St. George's, North
Dutch Church, Middle Dutch Church—used as the Post Office at this time,
and Trinity Church) only Trinity is still standing. The East River is in the
left background as it appeared prior to erection of the Brooklyn Bridge.

This color insert of *Lower Broadway* is typical of early 19th century
interior views of cities.

BROAD WAY FROM THE BOWLING GREEN

Richmond, Va., 1852.

On Stone by F. Palmer. A 38 x 21 colored lithograph taken from Manchester on the south side of the James River and showing Mayo's Bridge and Island in the center. Richmond was founded in 1733 and became the state capitol in 1779. In 1781 the British burned warehouses and public buildings, so most of the structures depicted were built after that time. The white building in the center background is the State Capitol, and the round dome to the right and rear of the Capitol is the Episcopal Church built in 1812. The first bridge above Mayo's Bridge is the Danville R. R. and at the left of the view is Hollywood Cemetery.

Atlanta, Georgia, 1864.

View of the public square on its capture by the Union Army, Sept. 2, 1864. A 12 x 21″ colored lithograph by Henry C. Eno of 37 Park Row, New York City. Delineated by Lieut. N. B. Arnold of the occupying 20th Army Corps. The insert views in the upper margin show (1) portrait of occupying General Slocum, (2) his headquarters and (3) fort at right of City Hall. The print is bordered by division and brigade battle flags and badges. Atlanta was founded in 1833 and owes its development to railroads. When Sherman's Union troops began their march "from Atlanta to the sea," Nov. 15, 1864, the city was almost completely burned.

Natchez, Miss., 1840.

From the old fort on the hill. A 21 x 13 colored lithograph by Risso & Browne, N. Y. Established as Fort Rosalie by the French in 1716, Natchez was long one of the chief frontier towns and later the capitol of Mississippi. The large house with columns, at the left is "Rosalie," a mansion used as the headquarters of General Grant during the Civil War and still standing. The building in the center is the courthouse and the steeple at the right of this view is the First Presbyterian Church, built in 1830 and still standing.

Providence, R. I., 1858.

View from the west bank of the river. A 33 x 16 lithograph by J. P. Newell. Founded in 1636 by Roger Williams, Providence colony was the first to have complete separation of church and state. At the time of this print, the city was switching from coastwise commerce to large manufactures in textiles, jewelry, silverware and foundry products. The tall steeple in the left center is First Congregational Church (1816); the structure with twin towers to the left is Central Congregational Church (1852); still further left is the slender, light colored spire of the First Baptist Church, 1775. The two towers to the extreme left are on the Union Depot, erected in 1848 and destroyed by fire in 1896.

Buffalo, New York, 1853.

J. W. Hill Del. J. H. Colen SC. A 39 x 23 tinted lithograph published by Smith Brothers & Co., 225 Fulton St., N. Y. and one of a series of "Views of American Cities." (The LADIES REPOSITORY for 1855 also has it reengraved and published in size 8 x 4"). The view shows Buffalo Creek in the foreground, with the Erie Canal on the left and the Main and Hamburg St. Canal on the right. First permanently settled in 1784 and burned in War of 1812, Buffalo developed rapidly after completion of Erie Canal in 1825 and development of Niagara power. Main Street runs up the middle of the print towards the background, with Washington Street just to the right. The print erroneously shows (near Terrace R. R.) St. Joseph's Catholic Cathedral with two spires (it never had but one). Prominent on the right side of Washington Street is the dark square tower of St. John's Episcopal Church, built in 1848 and demolished in 1906 to make way for the Statler Hotel.

Salem, Mass., 1853.

A 38 x 22 colored lithograph published by Smith Brothers & Co., New York. Founded in 1626 on a peninsula formed by two rivers entering the Atlantic, Salem enjoyed a virtual monopoly of the China Trade until the War of 1812. During the era of this print, its clipper ships were famous; but shortly thereafter larger ocean going vessels could not make its comparatively shallow harbor, and trade declined. This has given us a town that today is still reminiscent of by-gone times. Across the foreground of the view is Harbor Street, and at right angles is Lafayette Street. The foreground corner building here is Lafayette Methodist Church, erected 1853 and remodeled 1893. The building with two square towers, near the water in the left center is the Boston and Maine Railway Depot, erected in 1847. Most churches indicated in the background and many houses shown are still standing.

Rochester, N. Y., 1850

The Upper Falls of the Genesee, from the Chasm below. A 10 x 12 lithograph from Appleton's Journal, showing some of the great flour mills of the period. Established in 1811 and connected by the Erie Canal in 1825, for many years—while the Genesee Valley was "America's principal wheatfield"—Rochester was called "The Flour City." Few of today's visitors to what is now "The Kodak City" ever get this view of the town which has grown above, across and over the falls that sparked its founding.

Baltimore, Maryland, 1852.

Drawn from nature on stone by E. Sachse. A 27 x 18″ colored lithograph published by Sachse & Co., Baltimore. The center foreground shows the Washington Monument, started in 1815, completed in 1829, and still standing. The street running down to the river is Charles St. On the right of this street is a large white building with dome and two circular turrets, the Roman Catholic cathedral just completed in 1851. In front of the Cathedral is a smaller building with a dome, the Unitarian Church built in 1817, and on the left side of Charles Street is the steeple of St. Paul Episcopal Church, destroyed by fire shortly after this print was made. Baltimore was founded in 1730. Its harbor with 100 miles of water front makes it a leading place of export. The foreground street running into the monument is Mount Vernon Place.

Nashville, Tenn., 1850.

An 18 x 12 colored lithograph. In 1780 Fort Nashboro was built on these bluffs above the Cumberland River, and although subjected to repeated Indian attack, the settlement grew to become the state capitol in 1843. The large building at the extreme left is the original medical department of the University of Nashville, now the site of a park for the children of South Nashville. The large building at the extreme right is the Southern Methodist Publishing House, which is no longer standing. The suspension bridge here shown was "very unwisely destroyed by the Confederate Army upon its evacuation of Nashville" (1862).

Alexandria, Va., 1867.

Bird's eye view published by Charles Magnus, 12 Frankfort St., New York. A 23 x 14 colored lithograph showing the town from the Potomac River, very much as originally laid out in 1749. In the Civil War era depicted Alexandria was the capitol of the loyal section of Virginia. Numerous historic buildings are still preserved, including Christ Church (where Washington was a vestryman). Carlyle House (where General Braddock organized his expedition against Fort Duquesne) and the Lee home ("Light Horse Harry" and Robert E. Lee).

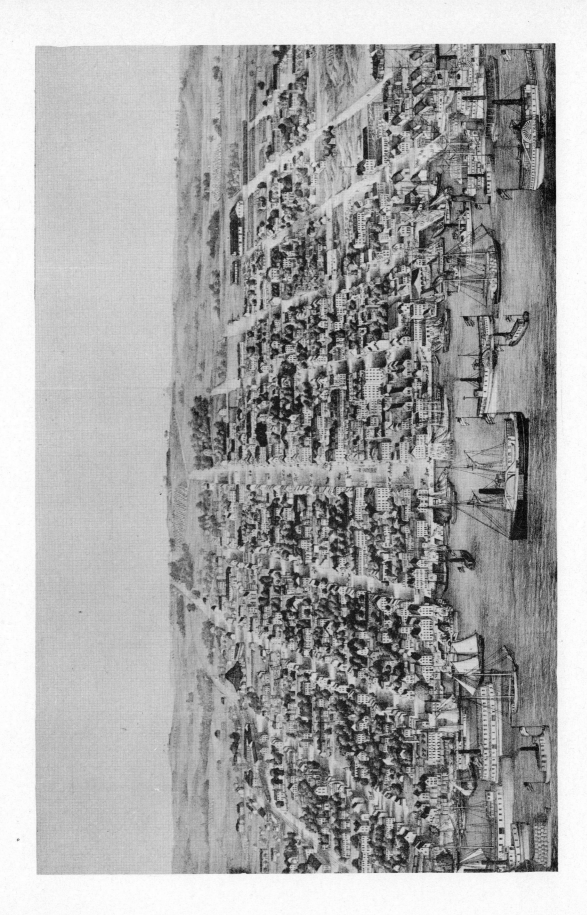

Portland, Maine, 1855.

To the citizens of Portland, this picture is most respectfully dedicated by the publishers. A 39 x 22 lithograph printed by Endicott & Co., New York City. Occupied as early as 1632 and repeatedly devastated by Indians (1676-1690), the present settlement dates from 1716. It was the capitol of Maine from 1820 to 1830 and owed its rapid growth to ship building facilities. The fine harbor (Fore river entering Casco Bay) and Cape Elizabeth is shown in the foreground of the print. The tall structure on Munjoy's Hill, at the right, is the Observatory (1807); the tower and cupola further to the right is the Middle Street Congregational Church, erected in 1788. Cupola and spire to the left of this indicate Baptist Church (1811) and Third Parish Church (1808). The cupola and tower further left is First Parish Church (1825).

Columbus, Ohio, 1865.

View from Capitol University. A 39 x 20 colored lithograph drawn and printed by E. Sache & Co., Baltimore, Md. The drawing shows the city stretched on both sides of the Scioto River, at its junction with the Olentangy. The west bank was first settled as Franklintown in 1797; but the major development came with the development of Columbus on the east bank several years later. In 1812 the city was selected for the territorial government, and in 1816 the legislature met in the newly erected capitol. The importance of railroads and the Ohio Canal are also indicated by this print.

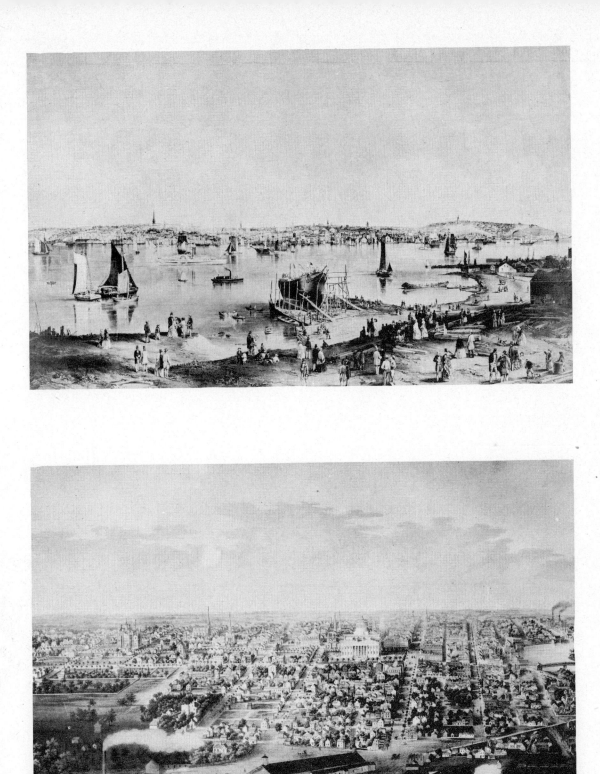

Augusta, Maine, 1853.

Drawn by F. B. Ladd. A 27 x 16 colored lithograph printed by F. Heppenhumer, 22 N. William St., N. Y. Actual settlement started in 1754 with the erection of a fort and occupied as the capitol of the state since 1831. Capitol building is shown on the high ground at extreme left of the print. The large church with square tower and cupola, at the right, is the Congregational Church, built in 1809 and destroyed by fire in 1864. At the extreme right is a covered bridge erected over the Kennebec River in 1827 and torn down in 1890. The railroad nearby first connected Augusta with Portland in 1851.

Wheeling, West Virginia, 1851.

A 30 x 19 colored lithograph by E. Sachse & Co., Baltimore, Md. Situated on the Ohio River and surrounded by vast coal fields, Wheeling early gained importance in manufactures and commerce. A fort was established here in 1774 and the town laid out in 1793. This view is from Chapline Hill and shows the original plants of many concerns still in business.

Concord, N. H., 1852.

A 26 x 15 colored lithograph printed in London, England from a painting by S. Harvey. The town was settled in 1725 and became the state capitol in 1808. The four large white cupolas in this view are, left to right; Unitarian Church, erected in 1829 and burned 1854; Baptist Church, erected 1825 and later remodeled; South Congregational Church, erected 1836 and burned 1859, and the State House, erected 1816 and enlarged and remodeled several times since.

Rutland, Vt., 1860.

From near the junction of East and Otter Creeks. A 37 x 25 colored lithograph "drawn, painted and published by Prof. F. Childs." The large white steeple in the center is the Congregational Church on Court Street, dedicated 1860. The factories to the left with smoke rising from chimneys are Lincoln Iron Works and Columbia Marble Works. Founded in 1770, by 1792 the courthouse (in front of Marble works) was built, and served until destroyed by fire in 1868.

Wilmington, Del., 1841.

Taken from the old ferry, Southeast. A 27 x 15 colored lithograph by T. Sinclair, Philadelphia. The site in Delaware was settled in 1638 by Swedish and Dutch colonists. Ship building soon became an important industry, and DuPont located here in 1802. There has also been much manufacturing. The view shows Ferry House at extreme right and shipyards at the extreme left. The building with the cupola, near the center of the view is the City Hall, built 1798 and later remodeled.

Trenton, N. J., 1851.

View from Morrisville, Pa. A 34 x 19 colored lithograph of Wm. Endicott & Co., New York. Settled in 1685 and named Trenton in 1714 this site at the head of navigation on the Delaware River became the state capitol in 1790. The view shows many early factories and public buildings. At the left is the domed state capitol and right of center is the Court House. In the foreground is the Pennsylvania Canal. The insert view shows *the Trenton cottage and R. R. taken from Cunningham's Tremont House.*

Old Swedish Church founded 1699

Harrisburg, Pa., 1856.

A 3 x 2 line drawing by J. W. Barber looking south across the Susquehanna. Featured is the new Pennsylvania Railroad bridge and the Old State House (1819-1897).

Wilmington, N. C., 1856.

A 3½ x 2 drawing by J. W. Barker reproduced from "Our Whole Country" and the earliest depiction we have found of this leading seaport of the state. Founded in 1730 and once the seat of the Royal Governor, in 1765 the town offered the first armed resistance to the Stamp Act. It was the center of blockade running in the Civil War and still continues as a shipping center. The view taken from the east side of Cape Fear River, opposite the foot of Market Street. On the right of the market is the tower of the Episcopal Church. The large building on the extreme left is the old Custom House.

Little Rock, Ark., 1856.

A 4 x 2 drawing from Barber and Howe's OUR WHOLE COUNTRY, showing the situation on the bluff that projects into the Arkansas River. The first white settlers came in 1812 and Little Rock became the territorial capitol in 1820. The building with the cupola at the right is the State House, begun in 1833 and completed in 1840.

Southern view of Harri...

West view of the central part of Wilmington N.C. from the ferry

Eastern view of Little Rock, Arkansas

Key West, Fla., 1855.

A 21 x 10 colored lithograph of Chandler & Co., Boston. This southern-most city in the United States was not permanently settled until 1822, being previously a rendevous for pirates and buccaneers. Situated on Key West Island, at the time of this view it had no rail or road connection with the mainland and many of its occupants were still engaged in salvage and naval stores. The view is reputedly taken from the "cupola of Browne & Curry's Warehouse."

New Orleans, La., 1951.

Bird's eye view drawn from nature on stone, by J. Bachman. A 31 x 21 colored lithograph of the city founded in 1718 by the French. The large white building in the center, with columns and domes is the newly erected St. Charles Hotel, destroyed by fire in 1894. The Customs House (1848) is the square white building to the right and near the Mississippi water front. Further right is the dome of the City Exchange, erected in 1841, used as the State Capitol from 1874 to 1882 and taken down in 1914. The prominent white building with tall central spire is the Cathedral of St. Louis, erected in 1789, remodeled as shown in 1850 and still standing.

Pittsburgh, Pa., 1849.

A 41 x 19 colored lithograph by Tappan and Bradford's, Boston. The view shows the golden triangle where the Allegheny and Monongahela Rivers join to form the Ohio River, with its early buildings and river traffic. The large domed building, to the right of center is the County Courthouse, completed in 1841 and destroyed by fire in 1882. To its left appears the Catholic Cathedral. The town at the left was originally (1787) called Allegheny and now (since 1906) "North Pittsburgh." Pittsburgh was originally Fort Duquesne (1755), and was formally laid out as a town in 1784.

Louisville, Ky., 1853.

An 8 x 4 line engraving taken by the LADIES REPOSITORY from a large and very rare lithographic view published 1853 by Smith Brothers & Co. The town was laid out in 1779 on a site opposite the falls of the Ohio River, but rapid growth did not come until years just prior to the date of this print. Steam navigation and construction of a canal around the falls are both shown herein.

Cleveland, Ohio

N.B. Shown as a colored insert is this 9 x 14 engraving of the late 1830's. Cleveland was laid out in 1796 and grew rapidly after the opening of the Ohio Canal (1830) and the coming of the railroads. This view is looking east from the corner of Bank and St. Clair Streets. From left to right are Cleveland Academy (1821), Trinity Church (1828), First Presbyterian Church (1834) and Court House (1828). All these early landmarks have long since disappeared.

Cincinnati, Ohio, 1855 (see page 53)

Cincinnati, Covington and Newport. A colored lithograph 16 x 11 showing the appearance of the Queen City from across the Ohio River. The tallest steeple in the left background is St. Peter's Cathedral, completed in 1844 and still standing. The round building on the hill at extreme rear right of the view is the old observatory, erected in 1845 by Nicholas Longworth. Cincinnati received its present name in 1790, in honor of the society of Revolutionary War Officers of that name. In the foreground of the picture, in the angle made by the junction of the Lieking and Ohio Rivers is the Newport Army Barracks as completed in 1855. Covington, Ky. is shown in the left foreground.

CLEVELAND, OHIO.

Chicago, Illinois, 1849.

As seen at the top of St. Mary's College. A. Kollner, Lith. of Philadelphia. Only known impression and a rarity of the Phelps-Stokes collection. The street in the foreground parallel with the lower margin is Superior Street. Running at right angles and into the background is Wolcott (now North State Street). Founded in the 1830's, first at the junction of north and south branches of the Chicago River (Wolf's Point), and later at its entrance to Lake Michigan (Fort Dearborn), Chicago grew rapidly as a manufacturing and trading center. It was almost completely destroyed by fire in 1871, all buildings shown here are gone. This view is looking south from Chicago Avenue towards the Chicago River (note shipmasts in background and lighthouse at extreme left).

Galena, Ill., 1855.

Whitefield's original views of North American cities, No. 37. A 36 x 19 lithograph of Endicott and Company, N. Y. and a prime example of an artist's attempt to depict the country's growth one hundred years ago. Galena was settled in 1820 and named after the extensive galena, or lead-sulphite deposits. The river in the center of the view is the Galena and the General U. S. Grant residence stands near the face of the bluff, overlooking the river.

A complete series of Whitefield's views is yet to be assembled. The one shown bears the highest numbering we know, but at least 50 are somewhere recorded as being made. The artist was born in England in 1816 and moved to this country in early youth. Most of his middle years (1845-1855) were dedicated to leaving a pictorial record of the most historically important cities of America, but these were never assembled as a unit. Views were issued in two principal series of lithographs, one in large folio and one in smaller size. In his later years (1875-1892) Whitefield made drawings of old and historic New England buildings, published as HOMES OF OUR ANCESTORS.

Indianapolis, Ind., 1854.

A 32 x 18 colored lithograph by E. Sachse & Co., Baltimore, Md. and now in the Garvan collection. In 1820 the town site was selected by a legislative commission as the location of the state capitol, and laid out with Main Streets radiating from a circular park, similar to the plan of Washington, D. C. The city grew very slowly, however, until the coming of railroads and highways after the Civil War. The print gives a bird's eye view of the thirty-year old city, as seen from the top of the Asylum for the Blind. It is surrounded at top and sides by miniature views of public buildings. At the bottom are two long views of Washington Street, looking north-east and south-east, respectively.

Kansas City, Mo., 1853.

A 6 x 4 line engraving taken from Dana's THE UNITED STATES ILLUSTRATED (N. Y. 1855). About 1800 French traders established a post where the Kansas River enters the Missouri. Kansas City proper was laid out in 1840 and the lots first sold in 1846. At the time of this print, the town had become the exclusive eastern terminus and outfitting post for the Santa Fe trail west to California. It grew rapidly after the Civil War as a livestock and grain center.

St. Louis, Mo., 1840.

Front Street. An 18 x 30 colored lithograph published by J. C. Wild. One of a series of Mississippi River views by this artist, showing the warehouses of the many outfitting firms. St. Louis was settled in 1764 by ("the first thirty") from New Orleans. First the center of fur trading, in the second half of the 19th century it developed iron, chemical, brewing and other industries.

Debuque, Iowa, 1859.

A 26 x 16 lithograph published by W. J. Gilbert, 110 Main St., Debuque. The principal view is an oval, showing the city as seen from across the Mississippi. The small views of residences and small buildings are in the margin. Debuque is the oldest settlement in Iowa. Its first settler, Julien Dubuque, was attracted to the spot in 1788 by its great lead deposits; but not until 1836 were the Indians moved from this location and the town laid out by authority of Congress. Many of the buildings shown here are still standing, including the Shot Tower (shown on the island and also as small view) and the City Hall and Market. What is called City High School in the print is actually the Dubuque Female Seminary, established and built in 1854 by Catherine Beecher (sister of Henry Ward and Harriet Beecher Stowe). One of the first institutions for the education of women in the west, it is now a Catholic girl's boarding school.

St. Paul, Minn., 1852.

City of St. Paul, Capitol of Minnesota, on stone by J. Queen. A 19 x 11 colored lithograph published by Thompson Ritchie. This site was purchased from the Sioux Indians in 1805 by Lieutenant Zebulon M. Pike, who first developed historic Fort Snelling nearby. First settled in 1838, the town was not incorporated until 1849. The large building with cupola in the left center elevation is the state capitol, erected in 1851 and destroyed by fire in 1881.

Omaha, Neb., 1867.

Looking north from Forest Hill. A 29 x 13 colored lithograph by Gast, Moeller & Co., St. Louis. Established as an Indian trading post in 1825, and entered by Mormon settlers in 1848, the town was formally laid out in 1854. The building with small cupola and flag, at the extreme left of the view, was the Territorial Capitol from 1857 to 1867. A short distance right are the steeples of the First Congregational Church (1857-1871) and Roman Catholic Church (1867-1894). The square building just to the right of these steeples is the first Court House (1866-1890). The large four-story Herndon House is shown at the foot of the wide street in the right center, built in 1858 and destroyed in recent times. Missouri River and Union Pacific Railroad are on the extreme right.

Tucson, Ariz., 1853.

Tucson, Sonora. A 7 x 4 tinted lithograph by Sarony and Co., N. Y. At this time the town on the Santa Cruz River belonged to Mexico and was composed mainly of Mission Church and military compound. Founded by the Spaniards in 1776, Tucson was finally acquired in 1854 by the Gadston purchase. It was occupied by Confederate troops in 1862 and was capitol of the territory from 1865 to 1875.

Pierre, S. D., 1843.

Fort Pierre (on the Missouri). A 7 x 5 lithograph from Maxmilian, TRAVELS IN THE INTERIOR OF NORTH AMERICA, (London, 1843-44). Situated on the west bank of the river opposite the present city of Pierre, this was an early trading post of the American Fur Company and named for Pierre Chouteau, a St. Louis fur trader. The property was acquired by the United States government in 1855 and laid out as a military reservation. The present capitol city of South Dakota was not established on the opposite (east) bank of the Missouri until 1880.

Sante Fe, N. M., 1850.

A 7 x 4 lithograph first appearing in Simpson, ROUTE FROM FT. SMITH TO SANTA FE. The city was founded by Spaniards about 1609, captured by the Pueblo Indians in 1680 and retaken by the Spaniards in 1690. With the advent of Mexican independence in 1821, it became the center of a flourishing trade over the Sante Fe trail. The United States took possession in the Mexican War (1846) and Fort Marcy, shown in the foreground of the print, was built shortly thereafter.

Fort Smith, Ark., 1853.

A 9 x 6 tinted lithograph by Sorony, Major and Knapp of New York. First erected in 1817 as a government post at the head of navigation of the Arkansas River, Fort Smith was long the chief point of distribution for western posts. The "fort" shown was built in 1840 just within the Arkansas border, and the town of that name was about 12 years old at the time of our picture. The fort was itself finally abandoned in 1871, but a part of the old structure yet remains.

Galveston, Texas, 1855.

Ansicht von Galvaston. A 16 x 10 colored lithograph printed in Dresden, Germany. Settled in 1837, this view is from the bay and shows the old cotton-loading wharves on the north side of the city. The church with two steeples on the left is the Catholic Cathedral, completed in 1847 and one of the few churches not destroyed by the hurricane and tidal wave of 1900. So many structures went down in that disaster it is all but impossible to check the accuracy of this early print.

San Antonio, Texas, 1852.

An 8 x 6 line engraving from the REPORT ON THE UNITED STATES AND MEXICO BOUNDARY SURVEY (1857). This first permanent white settlement in Texas dates from 1718. San Antonio was an important military post throughout the days of Spanish and Mexican rules. Captured by a small band of Texas revolutionaries in 1835, it was scene of "remember the Alamo" massacre upon its recapture by Santa Anna. The view shows the Military Plaza some time after Texas became a part of the United States. The prominent building with the dome and tower is the Church of San Fernardo, erected 1734-49 and restored 1828-41. The present edifice of that name is a replacement started in 1868.

Oklahoma City, Okla., 1890.

First house commenced April 22, 1889—a city of 10 months. A 29 x 15 colored lithograph by A. E. Downs, Boston. Occupied by Indians during the greater part of the 19th Century and known as the Indian Territory, the western half was thrown open to white settlers at noon April 22, 1889. It is reported that over 5,000 settlers dashed across the border and began settling this site on the North Canadian River that same day. The town was incorporated in 1890 and became state capitol in 1910. Shown prominently in foreground is the Sante Fe Railroad and the Army encampment that kept order in the tumultuous founding days.

OKLAHOMA CITY,
INDIAN TERRITORY.
1890.

Grand Forks, N. D., 1873.

While early 19th century trading posts were erected near this site on the Red River, the first real settlers did not arrive until 1871. The city was chartered ten years later, when the Northern Pacific R. R. reached it. This view is from a 3 x 6 drawing made in 1873 and is presumably seen from the outskirts, where now stands the University of South Dakota.

Rock Island, Ill., 1860

A 6 x 4 drawing from Appleton's Journal shows the arsenal of this great mid-western fortress for holding the Upper Mississippi. Important cities (Davenport, Iowa, and Rock Island, Illinois) grew up on the eastern and western shores opposite the military stronghold.

Madison, Wisc., 1855.

Taken from the water cure, south side of Lake Menona. A 21 x 12 sepia lithograph by C. Curiers, N. Y. This picturesque site on a narrow strip of land between Lake Menona (foreground) and Lake Mendota (background) was selected in 1836 as the territorial capitol, and building began the next year. Shown at the extreme left are the early buildings of the University of Wisconsin. The building with the dome, in the center of the view is the State Capitol, occupied until 1863, when it was torn down to make way for the present structure.

Milwaukee, Wisc., 1860.

A 12 x 9 line engraving by A. F. Waud. The site on Lake Michigan was first occupied by white settlers in 1818 and incorporated as a town in 1837. German immigration begun near this time gave the city its major industry of brewing and its characteristic architecture. The houses in the foreground are typical residences of the area in cream-colored brick. Beyond the Court House and many church spires can be seen something of the early brewing establishments with Lake Michigan in the background.

Detroit, Mich., 1870.

A 10 x 7 engraving from Appleton's Journal. Of all the five large cities on the Great Lakes, Detroit alone possesses claims to considerable antiquity. It was a French settlement from 1701 to 1760, under British rule from 1760 to 1796 and the state capitol until 1848. The old state capitol is shown in this view, a domed building surrounded by trees. It was built in 1823, later served as a High School and still later was the first Public Library. St. Anne's Catholic Church is also shown in the view. It was built in 1818 and torn down in 1886. Prominent in the right foreground is the Michigan R. R., connecting the city with the rest of the country by rails as well as by water.

Denver, Colorado, 1865.

Denver, City of the Plains. A 16 x 18 colored lithograph by J. Bien, N. Y. The first settlers came in 1857, and when gold was discovered the next year, it grew rapidly to become the territorial capitol. The building with square tower and pinnacles in the right center of the view is at what is now Lawrence and 14th Street; it was used by the Methodist Church from 1864 to 1887. The two-and-a-half story building to the left is the Colorado Seminary (1864) which later became the University of Denver. The lower house of the Colorado legislature first met here in 1867. The building with the square tower and flag (right background) is the United States Mint, and the large building to the left of it is Broadwell House, one of the most famous of early western hotels.

Lawrence, Kansas, 1860.

Looking northeast from the grounds of the University. An 18 x 14 lithograph of the town founded in 1854 by New England abolitionists. Its "underground Railroad" was the object of many raids by pro-slavery advocates from Missouri. At the extreme left is the Congregational Church, with the Unitarian Church in the left foreground. The large four story structure in the left background is the early Eldredge House and a steamer is shown on the Kansas River to the right. The stone masons in the foreground are presumably working on the first buildings of what became the State University.

Salt Lake City, Utah, 1870.

A 12½ x 8½ colored lithograph by Currier & Ives (Peters 4225). While this famous firm issued many prints of American cities, defects as are noted in this example are fairly typical: (1) the rendering is sketchy and the coloring crude; (2) there are many prominent inaccuracies such as too great proximity to Salt Lake, and the position of the Mormon Tabernacle. For such reasons, few Curriers are included in this book.

Salt Lake City was founded in 1847 by Brigham Young at the base of the Wasatch Mountains and twenty miles from the lake. The first Mormon tabernacle was erected in 1851 and demolished about 1870 to make way for the second and larger structure shown in the center of the picture.

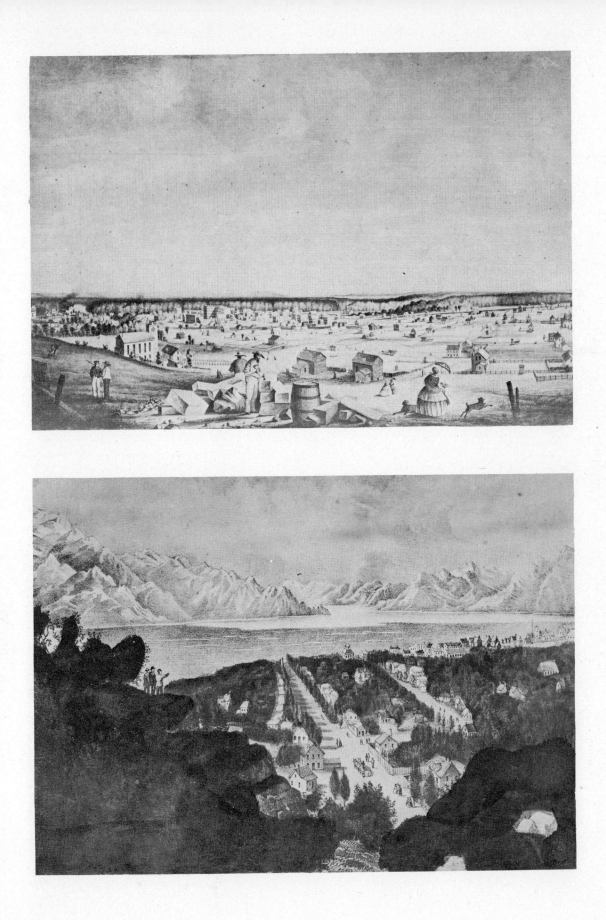

Virginia City, Nev., 1861.

A 27 x 18 lithograph with 30 small views of buildings in the margins. With the discovery of the famed Comstock Lode in 1859, the silvered hills on the eastern slope of Mount Davidson became a feverish clutter of shacks and saloons. At the time of this picture, there were 25,000 inhabitants. But here was one city where prophecy of limitless expansion went wrong. The mines petered out and Virginia City (named in honor of miner James Finney, known as "Old Virginny") became a ghost town. This and other mining town views were apparently published in San Francisco to be sent back to the home-folks in the east. The New York Public Library's print bears this pencilled notation "to Catherine Clark from her affectionate brother . . . boards here on the map marked thus, LL."

Helena, Montana, 1865.

Sketch after Nature by G. R. Bichler. A 19 x 30 colored lithograph by Herline & Hensel, Philadelphia. Founded in 1864 as LAST CHANCE GULCH with discovery of gold and silver, at the time of this picture, the population was 7500. The territorial government was moved here in the 1870's and the first railroad arrived in 1883. *(Courtesy N. Y. Hist. Soc.)*

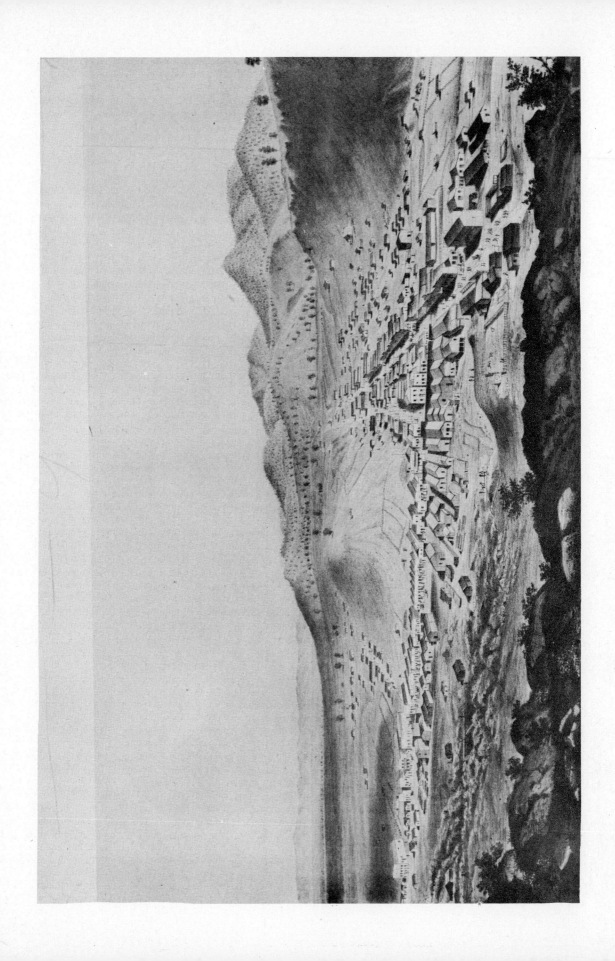

Laramie, Wyoming, 1842.

An 8 x 3 lithograph from the report of the Fremont Expedition of 1842. Old Fort Laramie is the site of the first permanent settlement near the confluence of the Laramie and Platte Rivers in Wyoming. It was erected in 1834 and rebuilt in 1836, serving as trading headquarters for the American Fur Company. The United States government did not acquire the property until 1849, and the town itself dates from after that period.

Boise, Idaho, 1850.

Fort on the Boise River. A 7 x 4 lithograph from an 1852 Congressional survey document (v. 3, 609). This was a Hudson Bay Company trading post preceding its occupation by the United States Army in 1863. The town was laid out the next year and made the territorial capitol.

Sacramento, Calif., 1849

From the foot of J Street, showing I, J and K Streets with the Sierra Nevadas in the distance. A 23 x 15 colored lithograph drawn December 20, 1849 by G. V. Cooper and lithographed by Wm. Endicott & Co., New York. The first white settler, Captain John A. Sutter came to this spot in 1839. When gold was discovered in the vicinty in 1848, settlers flocked to the spot and Sacramento, the future capital of California, developed overnight. The river boats shown in the foreground constitute an interesting feature of this rare and valuable print. Several smaller size copies exist.

Monterey, Calif., 1850

A 4 x 6 lithograph published by H. I. Meyer, New York. This beautiful bay site 90 miles southeast of San Francisco was named in 1602 and settled by the Spaniards in 1770. The city was long the capital of California under Spanish and Mexican rule. In 1849, three years after it was taken by the Americans, the first legislature of the State of California met in the large building here.

San Francisco, Calif., 1849.

Drawn on the spot by Henry Firks. A 32 x 13 colored lithograph printed by T. Sinclair, 101 Chestnut St., Philadelphia, Pa. This shows the site just after the discovery of gold, when it was being transformed from the tiny Spanish village of Yerba Beuna (founded 1776) to the busy American town of San Francisco. One of the artist's principal interest was the Clipper Ships in the harbor, to which there are numbered references in the lower margin. Early views of San Francisco are as interesting as rare, since the earthquake and fire of 1906 destroyed the early buildings.

Los Angeles, Calif., 1853.

A 9 x 6 colored lithograph from the War Department's REPORTS OF EXPLORATIONS AND SURVEYS (1855-60, v. 5, pt. 1). The first white settlement was established on this site by pious Spanish pioneers in 1781. Under Mexican rule until (1846) the city alternated with Monterey as capitol of California. This is the earliest known printed view in existence. The church in the left-middle distance is that of Our Lady of the Angels, erected in 1818, and remodeled (1861) after this drawing was made.

Portland, Ore., 1858.

A 34 x 19 lithograph by Kuchel & Dresel and the earliest recorded print of the town founded in 1845 at the confluence of the Willamette River with the Columbia. The view is from the east bank of the Willamette River and shows early lumber mills, the original Congregational Church (1851-1871) and the first public school, built in 1856-58. The general view of the city is surrounded by many small views of residences and business establishments.

Seattle, Washington, 1874.

A 19 x 49 water color drawing in the Phelps-Stokes collection that shows the city (founded 1851) just entering its third decade, with the skeleton of its present structure discernable. The view is taken from the western slope of Renton Hill, looking across Puget Sound to the Olympic Mountains. Straits leading to Pacific Ocean are to the right, with Magnolia Bluff and Danny Hill at the extreme right. West Seattle lies across the bay to the left, also the "tide lands" now filled in by successive regrades which removed tops of most of Seattle's hills. Wide avenue which runs from left foreground to waterfront is Yesler Way. The First Baptist Church is on the high ground to the right. The domed building in the extreme right background was the first home (1861) of the University of Washington and replaced in 1907 by business structures.

Tacoma, Wash., 1884.

A 32 x 12 lithograph published by J. J. Stoner, Madison, Wis. with 31 numbered references and 24 names and addresses of business firms in the lower margins, this is typical of the "booster prints" of the late 19th century. The Hudson Bay Company established a trading post here in 1822, but Tacoma usually dates its development from the arrival of Gen. McCarver from Portland in 1868 and the establishment of the Northern Pacific's Terminal in 1873.

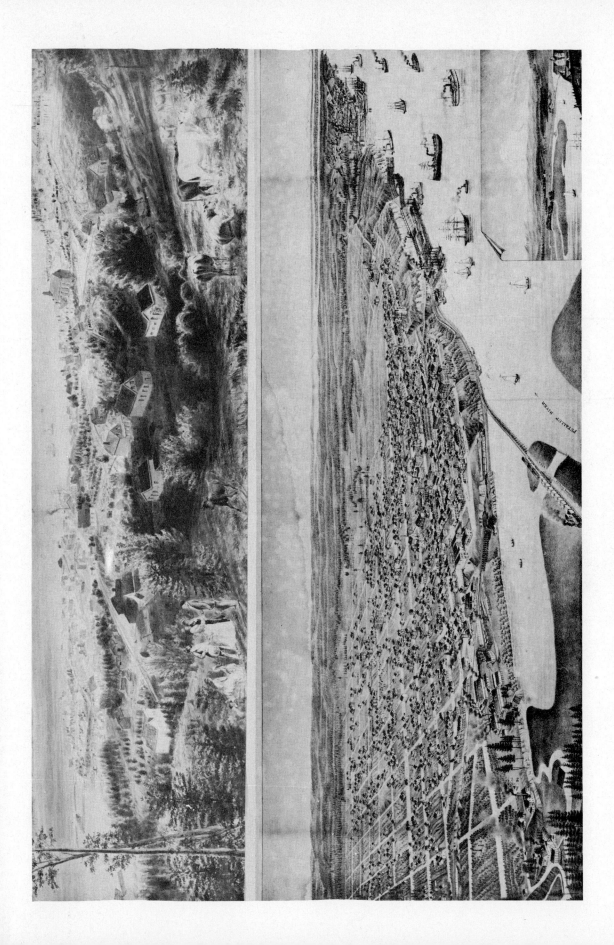

INDEX OF CITIES